Milwaukee

WISCONSIN

A PHOTOGRAPHIC PORTRAIT

Photography by Peter and Renée Skiba

Narrative by Anne Bingham

First published in the United States of America by:

Twin Lights Publishers, Inc.
8 Hale Street
Rockport, Massachusetts 01966
Telephone: (978) 546-7398
http://www.twinlightspub.com

ISBN: 1-885435-89-4
ISBN: 978-1-885435-89-7

Jacket front:
Mackie Building

Jacket back:
Water Tower near Lake Michigan

Frontispiece:
Sixth Street Viaduct

Opposite:
Ancient Rivalry

A statue of Solomon Juneau, who established the settlement that later became Milwaukee, overlooks Juneau Park on Milwaukee's east side. The buildings on the right are University Club Tower, the highest residential building in Wisconsin, and Kilbourn Tower, named after a Juneau rival, Byron Kilbourn, who established a competing town across the Milwaukee River. Kilbourntown joined Milwaukee in 1846.

Book design by:
LJ Lindhurst
www.w-rabbit.com

Printed in China

INTRODUCTION

*T*he exact meaning of the word *Milwaukee* is uncertain, but one of the traditional interpretations is "rich beautiful land," and that's what French fur trader Solomon Juneau must have thought when he arrived in 1833. Juneau built the first permanent European settlement between the shore of Lake Michigan and the east bank of the Milwaukee River, and the rest is history. His small village grew into Wisconsin's largest city—and residents and visitors alike continue to gather for the city's wealth of entertainment and recreational opportunities, many of them in vicinity of Juneau's first home.

The city's expansive Lake Michigan shoreline provides visitors with easy access to its museums, parks, and the first lake schooner built in Milwaukee in more than a hundred years. The lake also is a spectacular backdrop for the city's festivals, including Summerfest, an eleven-day music event on the lakefront that draws acts and audiences from around the world, and ethnic festivals renowned for their food, music, traditions, and crafts.

The food traditions brought to Milwaukee, often by European immigrants, are part of the city's distinctive charm. The Friday fish fry has reached far beyond its Catholic and Orthodox church roots to become the official start of the weekend for visitors as well as residents. National brands of soft-serve ice cream never quite caught on here, the taste melting in comparison to the rich frozen custard served at drive-in stands throughout the area.

Many of the industries that employed Milwaukee's early residents still maintain headquarters and factories in town, often on their original sites, and open their doors for tours. A strong tradition of historic preservation has saved many 19th- and early 20th-century homes, business structures, and entire neighborhoods for future generations. Many structures and neighborhoods are fully restored to their former glory or sensitively adapted to contemporary use. Contemporary buildings have developed their own distinctive style, both complementing and providing counterpoints to their vintage neighbors.

The photographs of Peter and Renée Skiba celebrate this vibrant juxtaposition of 21st-century exuberance rising from a city built on Old World charm and New World energy.

Iron Block Building

The Iron Block Building is constructed of wood and brick; the cast-iron façade is the reason for its name. The building is one of the few structures of its type remaining in the United States. Cast in sections at a New York foundry, the façade was transported to Milwaukee by ship; installation took place in 1861.

Sports Centers a Century Apart *(top)*

The walls of the Bradley Center sports complex, which opened in 1988, reflect Turner Hall, an 1882 clubhouse built by German immigrants to promote physical and mental fitness. One of the few surviving American Turner buildings, the clubhouse has hosted gymnastics classes for more than 120 years; it also sponsors community forums and serves a legendary Friday fish fry.

Northwestern Mutual Building *(bottom)*

Milwaukee is the home of one of the largest United States life insurance companies, Northwestern Mutual. Founded in 1857 in Janesville, the company moved to Milwaukee two years later and has stayed ever since. The current headquarters building on East Wisconsin Avenue, built in 1914, was modeled on a Roman temple to assure policyholders of the company's stability.

Wisconsin's Tallest Building *(above)*

At 601 feet, the 42-floor U.S. Bank Center is Wisconsin's tallest building, topping Milwaukee City Hall by some 200 feet. Completed in 1973 as the headquarters of what was then First Wisconsin National Bank, the structure is primarily glass (there are 5,000 windows and a galleria-style lobby), aluminum, and travertine marble.

Mitchell Building *(opposite)*

Built in 1876, the Mitchell Building on East Michigan Street is one of the country's finest examples of French Second Empire commercial architecture. The developer was Alexander Mitchell, a banker, railroad investor, and lumberman who was the father of General William "Billy" Mitchell, for whom Milwaukee's airport is named.

Next Door Neighbor *(above)*

Built next door to the Mitchell Building three years later, and designed by the same architect, Edward Townsend Mix, for Alexander Mitchell, the Mackie Building originally housed offices for the Chamber of Commerce and commodities traders, as well as a trading room. The High Italianate façade includes carved heads of bulls and bears.

New Life for an Old Treasure *(opposite, top)*

An inlaid wood panel on the floor commemorates the 1983 restoration of the 10,000-square foot Grain Exchange Trading Room in the Mackie Building. For a brief period after the Civil War, Milwaukee led the world in the amount of grain it exported, and this room served as the world's first commodities trading pit.

Tribute to Milwaukee Workers *(opposite, bottom)*

A roundel high on the west wall is based on Wisconsin's State Seal and depicts a sailor and a laborer, who represent marine and land-based industry. The badger at the top of the shield originally referred to Wisconsin's lead miners, who first were housed in caves they called badger dens. Eventually Wisconsin became known as the Badger State.

Henry S. Reuss Federal Plaza

The modernist, multi-faceted glass exterior
of the Henry S. Reuss Federal Plaza provides
a dramatic backdrop for Helaine Blumfield's
Family, a five-form abstract sculpture of
Norwegian blue granite that complements the
building's cobalt trim. The open-air atrium
and the building's lobby are the setting for
performances and exhibits throughout the
year.

South Shore Water Frolics

Lakefront fireworks on the eve of Independence Day draw tens of thousands of viewers to parks, hillsides, and high-rise buildings around the harbor. Many families arrive early in the morning with lawn chairs, grills, coolers, and blankets to stake out their spot. This view is from Bay View Park near the South Shore Yacht Club.

Milwaukee County Courthouse

The Neoclassical Revival Milwaukee County Courthouse was completed in 1931 following a nationwide design competition. The 11-story Courthouse overlooks the broad pedestrian plaza of MacArthur Square, dedicated to General Douglas MacArthur; the general had attended West Division High School, which is now Milwaukee High School of the Arts. The blue flag on the left is the Wisconsin state flag.

U.S. Courthouse and Federal Building

The Romanesque U.S. Courthouse and Federal Building, completed in 1899, occupies a full city block on East Wisconsin Avenue. The façade is Maine granite and the turrets are sheathed in copper. The building is still used for its original purpose, housing U.S. Department of Justice federal district courtrooms and offices.

Weather Beacon *(opposite)*

Constructed as the headquarters for the city's gas utility, this art deco structure of multicolored brick still is known locally as the Gas Building. The current owners maintain the rooftop gas-flame-shaped weather beacon, which changes color depending on the weather forecast: red for warm, gold for cold, blue for no change, and "a flickering flame for snow or rain."

Milwaukee City Hall *(above and right)*

The exterior renovation of Milwaukee's Flemish Renaissance City Hall is expected to be completed by 2010; the interior displays fine examples of craftsmanship. The Seal of Wisconsin at the entrance to the third-floor Council Chambers dates to a 1930s WPA art project. The Council Chambers wood-paneled walls are carved with 19th-century classical motifs.

Neighbors in White

The 16-story Cudahy Tower, built by meat-packer Patrick Cudahy in 1909, was one of Milwaukee's first lakefront high-rise apartment buildings. The 36-story University Club Tower behind it is the state's tallest residential building; it was designed to complement the Cudahy as well as two other buildings in white: the U.S. Bank Center and the Milwaukee Art Museum's Calatrava addition.

The Bradley Center

Named for Harry Lynde Bradley, a co-founder and chairman of the Allen-Bradley Company the Bradley Center is home to the Milwaukee Bucks, an NBA basketball team; the Milwaukee Admirals, an NHL hockey team; and the Marquette University Golden Eagles basketball team. The facility hosts around 180 events a year, including concerts and community events in addition to sports.

Cedar Creek Winery *(opposite)*

A restored woolen mill in Cedarburg, about 20 miles northwest of downtown Milwaukee, includes shops and a winery owned by the Wollersheim family. The winery is open for tours and wine tastings. While some grapes used in the wines are grown in milder climates such as Washington state, all Cedar Creek wines are cask-aged in the mill's limestone cellars.

Trolley Ride *(above)*

Replicas of trackless trolley cars from the early 20th century provide downtown transportation during the summer months to shopping, museums, restaurants, parks, concerts, lakefront festivals, and other attractions. Year-round, they are a frequent sight on area streets as they transport guests to weddings, proms, convention tours, and other special events.

21

Pabst Theater *(opposite)*

Designed to resemble a European opera house, the Pabst Theater opened just eleven months after a fire destroyed another theater also owned by brewer Frederick Pabst on the same site. The 300-seat theater is used for music, theater, opera, and dance productions that are especially suited for the theater's traditional proscenium stage, such as Dickens' "A Christmas Carol."

Brady Street *(above)*

The nine blocks of Brady Street stretch from the Milwaukee River to a pedestrian bridge leading down the bluff to the Lake Michigan shore, and encompass nearly 175 years of history. Most of the buildings were constructed between the Civil War and 1930 for working-class immigrants. Today, Brady Street is a shopping and dining destination.

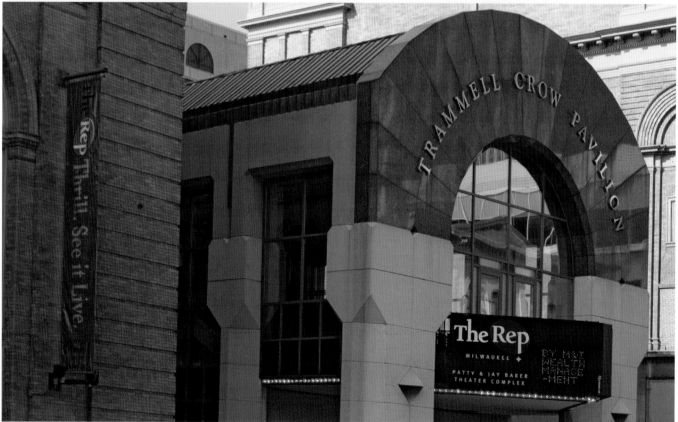

Classic Library Building *(opposite, top)*

The main part of the Milwaukee Central Public Library was completed in 1898 in the Classical Revival style from limestone quarried in Bedford, IN, the same material used in the Milwaukee County Courthouse. Of special note are mosaic floors under the entrance rotunda and a wide stone staircase. The library's special collections include Great Lakes shipping documents and photographs.

Theater District *(opposite, bottom)*

Milwaukee Repertory Theater, a resident company founded in 1954, has three performance spaces inside the Patty and Jay Baker Theater Complex, a converted power-generating plant. The Rep's theaters include the Quadracci Powerhouse, the 218-seat Stiemke Theater for intimate drama; and Stackner Cabaret, a restaurant-and-bar venue that focuses on music-based pieces.

History of Human Work *(above)*

Exhibits in the galleries at the Grohmann Museum on the campus of the Milwaukee School of Engineering explore the evolution of human work. Exhibits include the development of farming, mining, crafts such as glassblowing, and work in the Industrial Age. The museum, which opened in 2007, also has a rooftop sculpture garden.

Betty Brinn Children's Museum *(opposite)*

Hands-on learning for children through age 10 is the focus of the Betty Brinn Children's Museum, which opened across the street from the Milwaukee Art Museum in 1995. Permanent exhibits include A Trading Place, a gallery of child-sized versions of area businesses that includes a grocery store, an auto service center, and a café.

Larger-than-Life Toy Train *(above)*

A replica of a Brio wooden train is large enough for children to play in. The engine has levers and dials for them to "operate" and the Cattle Wagon includes a wooden cow and a bucket for her milk. The exhibit also has a traditionally sized Brio train track layout complete with a red suspension bridge and hills.

Body Language *(right)*

Little visitors can learn how their body uses food by crawling through a giant digestion tunnel in the My Body Works exhibit. A huge human heart teaches the concept of blood circulation as children slide through it. Another section of the exhibit reinforces healthy lifestyle choices and offers children the chance to practice calling 9-1-1.

Milwaukee County Historical Society *(above)*

The headquarters of the Milwaukee County Historical Society originally opened in 1913 as the Second Ward Savings Bank; the Society moved into the Beaux Arts building in 1965. Located in Pere Marquette Park on the banks of the Milwaukee River, the building's research library includes territorial and federal census data and other records useful for genealogy research.

Architecture Large and Small *(opposite, top)*

The main floor of the Historical Society building is decorated in French Renaissance style and was originally two stories high; the mezzanine is a later addition. The model of Milwaukee City Hall is on loan from the local chapter of the American Institute of Architects, who commissioned its construction from Lego toy bricks for a children's exhibit at Summerfest.

Commercial Detail *(opposite, bottom)*

Winged lions flank an urn in this panel from a wood-and-terra cotta fireplace in the County Historical Society's headquarters. The fireplace, originally three-sided, once stood in the shoe department of a T. A. Chapman Department Store, a local company that closed in the early 1980s. The Society's business archives include incorporation records for firms founded from 1872 to 1960.

Milwaukee Public Market *(above and left)*

Produce has been sold on Commission Row in the Third Ward for over a century. The wholesalers of the past have moved elsewhere, but the tradition of fresh food continues, with a score of private vendors at the Milwaukee Public Market offering a selection of fruit and vegetables as well as meat, fish, flowers, breads, and other specialty and gourmet items. Open seven days a week year-round, from morning coffee to after-work take-out, the Market has seasonal outdoor stalls and a mezzanine level for on-site enjoyment of sandwiches, salads, and soups.

Riverwalk *(above and right)*

Developed to enhance access to the Milwaukee River, Riverwalk consists of three miles of paved paths and boardwalk through upscale residential neighborhoods, shopping and dining areas, and recreational facilities in downtown and the Historic Third Ward. Many restaurants have open-air plazas for riverfront dining, and the area is a popular destination for recreational boaters. The view above looks south from the Wells Street bridge; the building with the dark glass façade is the Chase Bank Building. At right, an enclosed sky bridge leads from the Grand Avenue Mall to the Chase Bank Building just beyond the right border of the photo.

Milwaukee's Niche Sports   *(above)*

There's more to the Milwaukee sports scene than football, basketball, and baseball. The first season for the Milwaukee Lake Park Lawn Bowl Club was in 1919. The Italian Community Center has an indoor court for a similar game, bocce ball, and several metropolitan curling clubs have organized since the Milwaukee Curling Club was founded in 1845.

North Point Water Tower   *(left)*

Built in 1873 to prevent ice from forming on the iron standpipe inside, the 175-foot North Point Water Tower was in service until a new pumping station opened in 1963. The standpipe absorbed pulsations from the engines pumping Lake Michigan water into city water mains. The copper-topped Victorian Gothic tower is constructed of Niagara limestone quarried in nearby Wauwatosa.

Alterra on the Lake *(above and right)*

One of the country's earliest water pollution control systems, the Milwaukee River Flushing Station on the lakefront north of downtown had the highest-capacity pump in the world—more than a half billion gallons daily—when it was constructed in 1888. Its purpose was to pump Lake Michigan water into the Milwaukee River to dilute sewer pollution. The Cream City Brick building now functions both as an interpretive center to teach about water management issues and as a café/deli in partnership with Alterra, a locally owned specialty coffee company. Alterra occupies two-thirds of the Station's area and offers alfresco dining on its terraces during warm weather. The remaining space contains the pumping facilities, still functional but no longer in use.

Microbrewing Makes Its Mark   *(above and left)*

Milwaukee's reputation as a beer-brewing capital is returning with the emergence of specialty microbreweries. Originating as a family beer-making adventure, Lakefront Brewery's first site was a former neighborhood bakery, but sales grew so rapidly Russ and Jim Klisch soon moved the firm to its current Commerce Street location in a renovated Milwaukee Electric Rail Car power plant. The craft brewery, whose products include year-round and seasonal beers and a gluten-free beer, was the first certified organic brewery in the nation. Brewery tours are available weekdays; a Friday fish fry in the brewery's Palm Garden includes polka music and atmosphere provided by a genuine Lawrence Welk bubble machine.

Miller's Original Brewery Site   *(opposite)*

Miller Brewing Company still occupies land that founder Frederick J. Miller leased in 1855 and then purchased from the Plank Road Brewery. Miller tours include a replica of the old brewery and a restored storage cave as well as the modern brew house. Visitors conclude their tour at the Bavarian-style Miller Inn for samples of beer or soft drinks.

Biking and Hiking Circuit *(above and left)*

The cyclists on this lakefront segment of the Oak Leaf Trail are able to circle Milwaukee County on the trail's hundred-plus miles of paved asphalt paths, scenic parkways, and designated city bike lanes. The well-signed trail has grown considerably from its initial length of 64 miles when it was established in 1939.

Riverfront Recreation *(above and right)*

The *Edelweiss* excursion boat, resting at its dock on the Milwaukee River, offers harbor tours for both walk-on passengers and group charters. At right, one of Milwaukee's 21 drawbridges opens to admit a sailboat into the river. In the background is Marine Terminal Lofts, one of the many condominium developments that have replaced, or been developed from, obsolete riverfront factories and warehouses in the old Third Ward neighborhood.

Commemorating Immigrants

The bronze statue "dedicated to the Valiant
Immigrant Mothers" stands in Cathedral
Square Park across from the Cathedral of
St. John the Evangelist, the site of one of the
city's first public squares. Created by Croatian
sculptor Ian Mestrovic, the statue commemorates the hardships experienced by immigrant
families in the early to mid-19th century.

Cathedral Old and New

The Neo-Baroque tower of the Catholic
Cathedral of St. John the Evangelist, one of the
city's oldest churches, has been a downtown
landmark since it replaced a shorter original
in 1893. The building's interior was gutted
by fire in 1935, but the tower survived. A
recent restoration reconfigured the cathedral's
interior and added an atrium and garden to
the north.

Ancient Chapel

Summer flowers provide a restful border for the plaza in front of the oldest building in the city, a 15th-century French oratory donated to Marquette University in 1964. Built in Lyon, France, around the time of St. Joan of Arc and associated with her in popular devotions of the region, the chapel today serves its original function as a site for prayer.

Glass in the French Tradition *(opposite)*

The four stained glass windows inside the St. Joan of Arc Chapel, modeled after colors in the windows of La Sainte-Chapelle in Paris, were commissioned in the 1920s to fit the original stone mullions and traceries. The chapel was attached to a French château on Long Island at the time.

St. Paul's Episcopal Church *(above)*

St. Paul's Episcopal Church, designed in Romanesque style by Edward Townsend Mix, was constructed with red Lake Superior sandstone from the Apostle Islands. Dedicated in 1884, the interior contains wrought iron features by Cyril Colnik and ten stained glass windows from the Tiffany Studios. Mix also designed two nearby churches, All Saints Episcopal Cathedral and Immanuel Presbyterian Church.

The Basilica of St. Josaphat   *(above and opposite)*

Polish immigrants and their descendants contributed much of the labor for building the Basilica, using some 200,000 tons of material from the condemned Chicago Post Office and Customs House. The church, dedicated in 1901, was proclaimed a "minor basilica" by Pope Pius XI in 1929 because of its preeminence as a regional center of devotion and its historic and architectural distinction. A full-scale restoration during the 1990s restored the interior to the original color and decorating scheme. The proportions of the dome, one of the largest in the world, match those of St. Peter's in Rome, on which it was modeled.

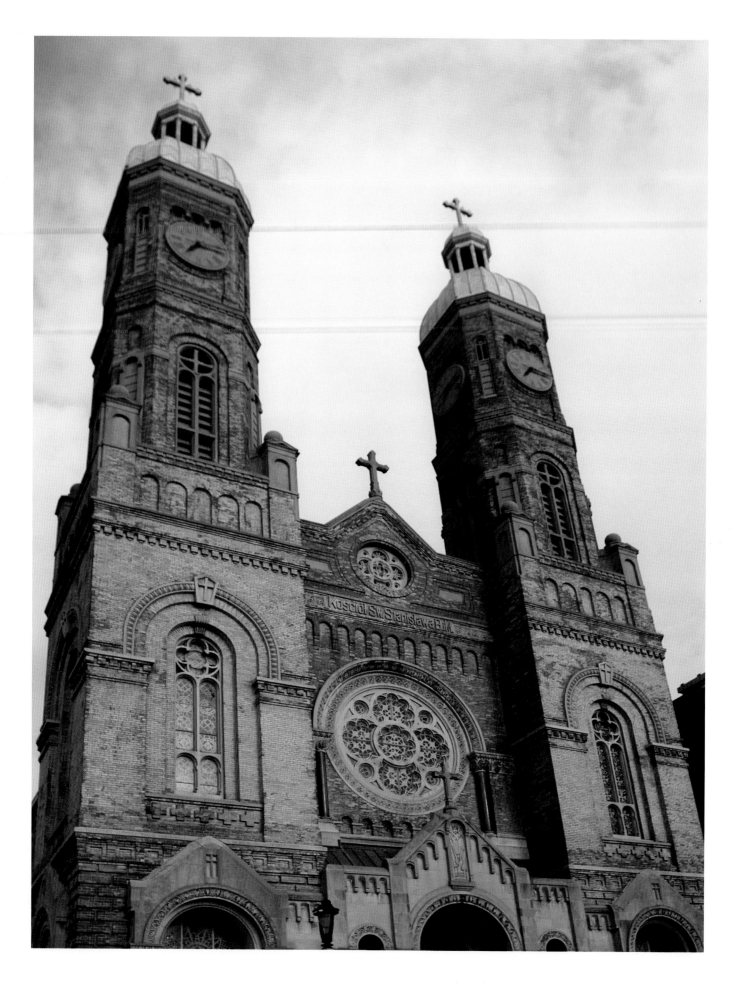

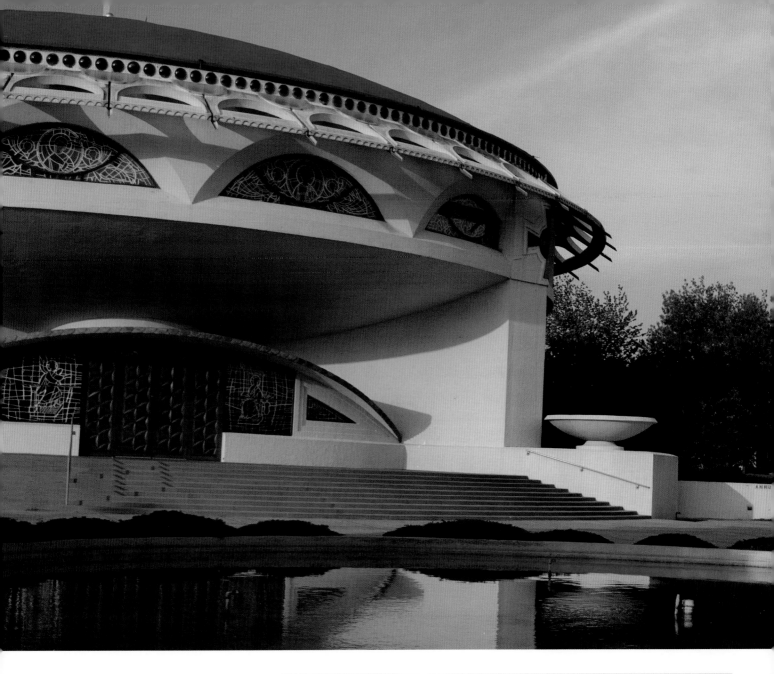

Twin Clock Towers *(opposite)*

St. Stanislaus Roman Catholic Church was
Milwaukee's first parish church for Polish-
speaking Catholics. Completed in 1873, it was
only the third Polish parish in the nation. Its
twin clock towers, originally copper-domed,
were covered with gold leaf in 1962. The
church's interior includes a mosaic of Our
Lady of Czestochowa, also known as the
Black Madonna, an image rooted deep in
Polish history.

Church of the Annunciation *(above and right)*

One of the last works by architect Frank Lloyd
Wright, a Wisconsin native, the Greek Orthodox Church of the Annunciation on the city's
northwest side is constructed of reinforced
concrete. The postmodern design is based on
a Greek cross inscribed on a circle; blue resin
covers the dome. The church was dedicated
in 1961.

Henry Maier Festival Park *(above and left)*

A central location for Milwaukee's Summerfest music festival and nearly a dozen ethnic and community celebrations, Henry Maier Festival Park on the downtown lakefront includes a 23,000-seat amphitheater and several other stages. At left, the yellow Summerfest Flag and the deep blue Wisconsin state flag flutter in the lake breeze among flags of the ethnic groups who host weekend festivals in the park, including, from left, Germany, Italy, and Poland. In addition to nation-specific festivals, the park also hosts regional festivals, including African World Festival, Arab World Fest, Mexican Fiesta, and Indian Summer.

Soaring above Summerfest *(above and right)*

Cable cars over Henry Maier Festival Park ferry riders high above Summerfest, an 11-day contemporary music festival billed as "the world's largest" with an estimated attendance of over one million people each year. The ethnic festivals focus on crafts, dancing, music of the past and present, and programs that discuss the groups' history in the area. At right, an exhibitor at Polish Fest demonstrates the art of *wycinanki,* intricate designs cut from paper.

World's Best Bikers

World-class cycling comes to the city each summer during the multi-category Point Premium Root Beer International Cycling Classic. The high-caliber bike series features both men's and women's Superweek Pro Tour races in 12 city centers throughout Eastern Wisconsin and northern Illinois, including several locations in the Greater Milwaukee area.

Milwaukee Rowing Club *(above)*

From spring through late autumn, rowing teams from the Milwaukee Rowing Club head for the Menomonee, Milwaukee, and Kinnickinnic rivers. Founded in 1894, the club's mission is to provide the broadest possible access to rowing opportunities and classes for community members age 14 and older, including college teams. The club's boathouse is located on Commerce Street

Lake Park *(opposite)*

Designed by Frederick Law Olmstead in the manner of a European park, Lake Park on the city's East Side has great open meadows alternating with woodland and paths leading to dramatic views of Lake Michigan. Two ravines near the south end of the park are spanned by bridges guarded by sandstone lions that have delighted generations of local children.

Mitchell Gallery of Flight *(opposite, top and bottom)*

A bust of General William "Billy" Mitchell stands near the entrance to Mitchell Gallery of Flight, a museum on the concession level of General Mitchell International Airport. The general was an early advocate of the military use of air power. The gallery contains exhibits on other aviators with Milwaukee ties, including Apollo 13 astronaut James Lovell, and a display related to a 1927 visit by Charles Lindbergh. The large portrait is another depiction of General Mitchell, for whom the airport is named. Suspended from the ceiling in the lower picture is a 1/36 scale model of the Graf Zeppelin II.

Milwaukee County War Memorial *(above)*

A mosaic of Roman numerals depicts the years of World War II and the Korean Conflict on the façade of the Milwaukee County War Memorial. Designed in the mid-1950s by Eero Saarinen to honor Milwaukee County's armed service members, the War Memorial includes a statue of Abraham Lincoln sculpted in 1934 by Gaetano Cecere.

High Above the Harbor

Visitors take in the harbor view from the balcony outside the Pilot House party room on the top floor of Discovery World, an interactive science and industry museum that opened in 2006. Part of the Pier Wisconsin lakefront education center, Discovery World is located between the Henry W. Maier Festival Park and the Milwaukee Art Museum.

Sailing Lessons

Sailors from the Milwaukee Community Sailing Center join other small craft docking near the Discovery World entrance. More than 100,000 people have taken sailing lessons through the Sailing Center since it was established in 1977 in a joint venture with Milwaukee County to make sailing accessible to all residents.

57

Discovery World   *(opposite, top and bottom)*

The water-themed area of Discovery World includes the *Challenge*, a life-sized replica of the first ship built especially for Great Lakes travel; guests are free to climb aboard and learn to steer using the pilot wheel and the rudder. The Reiman Aquariums have both salt water and fresh water habitats for fish. Fish float over the ceiling of a tunnel through one of the large aquariums; in another area, guests can pet a shark or a sting ray. A regional aquarium in the shape of the Great Lakes includes an overhead display of thunder, lightning, and rain.

Molecule of Life   *(above)*

Guests in the science and technology area of Discovery World ascend the double-helix staircase, which spirals around a continually expanding and shrinking model of a DNA molecule. The eight-sided clock faces to the left of the staircase are replicas of the ones on the Allen-Bradley Clock Tower.

Milwaukee Public Museum *(above)*

With 150,000 feet of exhibit space that
includes dinosaur skeletons, a 19th-century
downtown Milwaukee Street, and a two-story
conservatory filled with live butterflies, Milwaukee Public Museum gives visitors an un-
derstanding of how people and animals have
lived in the natural world through the ages.
The museum began in an 1851 classroom; its
current facility was completed in 1962.

Other Times, Other Places

Three-dimensional dioramas throughout the museum bring ancient scenes to life. The Pacific Islands exhibit on the third floor includes depictions of traditional customs in Papua New Guinea, Samoa, and Easter Island. Four African dioramas also on the third floor depict scenes from the savanna bush, a water hole, a salt lick in a bamboo forest, and Masai hunters protecting their cattle from a lion. A contemporary diorama depicts a life-sized, 37-member Native American powwow based on life casts of contemporary members of the seven tribes in Wisconsin.

Haggerty Museum of Art

A kiosk announcing current exhibits duplicates an architectural motif from the exterior of the Haggerty Museum of Art. Located on the campus of Marquette University, the museum is named for a Marquette alumnus who was a co-founder of Texas Instruments, Patrick E. Haggerty, and his wife Beatrice. The building opened in 1984.

Classic Paintings

Old World paintings in the Haggerty's permanent collection are displayed in a salon setting, much as they would have been in a European palace. The museum, which is free and open to the public, has four galleries and more than 4,000 works of art in its permanent collection, including paintings, sculpture, and installations of video art.

Performing Arts Setting

The Marcus Center for the Performing Arts provides venues in several sizes for cultural events and performances of music, drama, and dance. Uihlein Hall seats more than 2,300; two smaller theaters provide more intimate audience experiences. An open-air pavilion on the Milwaukee River has sheltered theater seating for summer performances.

Memorial in Bronze   *(top)*

Laureate, a 14-foot cast bronze work by Abstract Expressionist sculptor Seymour Lipton, faces the Milwaukee River on the west side of the Marcus Center. Dedicated in 1969, the year the center opened, the sculpture was commissioned by the Allen-Bradley Company in memory of co-founder Harry Lynde Bradley, who also was a prominent collector of modern sculpture.

Reception Area   *(bottom)*

Grand staircases of travertine marble lead to the first and third floors on the building's north and south sides. The Magin Lounge and the Anello Atrium on the second floor have high glass walls that provide a dramatic view of the city; in addition to hosting theater-goers at intermission, the atrium and lounge are popular for receptions and business gatherings.

Villa Terrace Decorative Arts Museum

Originally the home of a manufacturing magnate Lloyd R. Smith of the A.O. Smith Company, this Italian Renaissance-style villa was completed in 1923. Its collections focus on fine and decorative arts from the 15th to 18th centuries. The formal garden pictured here, viewed from Lincoln Memorial Drive, recreates a formal Tuscan garden of the 16th century, and includes a water stairway and two secret gardens.

The Captain Frederick Pabst Mansion

Steamboat captain-turned-brewer Frederick
Pabst built this Flemish Renaissance Revival
home in 1890–93. The attached pavilion
visible in the far right of the photo originally
stood in a Pabst beer garden at the 1892
Columbian exhibition in Chicago. The mansion, open to the public for tours, is owned
by a preservation group that has restored the
building and grounds.

Young Captain Pabst *(top)*

A photo on a table in Captain Pabst's study shows the businessman in his mid-thirties. Most of the materials used to construct the home, including the custom-carved oak woodwork visible in this picture, came from local sources. The drinking horns flanking the Henry Rauschen landscape over the fireplace were presented to Pabst by a business associate.

Failsafe Lighting *(bottom)*

Gold leaf highlights the ceiling decorations in the Pabsts' birch-paneled dining room. The Louis XV-style chandelier, made in Milwaukee, uses three forms of illumination: gas, electricity, and kerosene. Electrical power was available only in the daytime when the home was built, so gas illumination was the standard for evening entertainment. Kerosene served as a backup.

Tomorrow's Performing Artists

The cheerful façade of Lincoln Center of the Arts Middle School advertises the arts-integrated curriculum within. Students in sixth, seventh, and eighth grades learn the fundamentals of music, drama, and dance, along with traditional academics. The school's performances are open to the public, and ticket prices are said to be among the best arts bargains in town.

Paintings in a Home Setting   *(opposite)*

Designed specifically to be a house museum, the Tudor-style Charles Allis Art Museum, built by Charles Allis of Allis-Chambers Corporation, holds a collection of 19th-century French and American paintings, including examples of the Barbizon and Hudson River schools. The building on Milwaukee's East Side was completed in 1911; a Great Hall added in the late 1990s tripled the space for exhibits and programming.

Golfing Destination   *(above and right)*

The golf course at Brown Deer Park, part of the Milwaukee County Park system, hosts the U.S. Bank Championship each summer. Located in the northern part of the county, the tournament is part of the annual PGA tour and has hosted golfing greats, including Tiger Woods in his rookie season. In all, Milwaukee County parks have 16 golf courses, ensuring that access to public courses is available throughout the metropolitan area.

Milwaukee's Tall Ship

More than 90,000 volunteer-hours over six years went into building the *S/V Denis Sullivan*, a reconstruction of a 1880s Great Lakes cargo ship. Launched in 2000, the 137-foot schooner, the first to be built in Milwaukee in over 100 years, is a floating classroom and research vessel commissioned by Pier Wisconsin to raise awareness of the Great Lakes and ocean ecosystem issues.

Customized Voyage *(above and right)*

Among the lakefront's summer water recreation offerings is a Sea Dog charter sail aboard Captain Bob De Vorse's 34-foot yacht *Blue Chip*. Operating out of McKinley Marina north of the Milwaukee Art Museum, sailing options can be customized to passengers' wishes, including 90-minute afternoon getaways, sunset, moonlight, and overnight cruises, and full-day sails. The *Blue Chip* is a 1991 Catalina cruising yacht with all required safety equipment, and can accommodate up to six passengers.

New State Park

Lakeshore State Park in Milwaukee Harbor, framed here by a footbridge from the mainland, includes a small watercraft beach for kayaks and canoes, boat slips for vessels up to 60 feet, fishing access, a short grass prairie habitat for grassland birds, and a multi-use trail that connects to the Hank Aaron State Trail and the Milwaukee County Oak Leaf Trail.

Milwaukee Art Museum

Established in 1957 from the merger of two private art institutions, the Milwaukee Art Museum was originally housed entirely in the War Memorial building. Additions over the years have culminated in the Quadracci Pavilion, above, designed by architect Santiago Calatrava, and the Burke Brise Soleil, a wing-like sunscreen that is raised during museum hours when weather permits.

Waiting for a Bite   *(top and bottom)*

Milwaukee Harbor is a center for both recreation and commercial navigation. Anglers hope to harvest some of the lake's game fish. Near shore and deep lake species in Lake Michigan include salmon, trout, bass, perch, pike, bullheads, and sturgeon. Excursion boats offer several tours a day during the milder months. Charter fishing also is available.

Distant Voyagers

Ocean-going vessels as well as lake freighters pass under the Hoan Bridge to reach the Port of Milwaukee. On a daily basis during the shipping season, the port handles steel, machinery, grain, coal, road salt, cement, asphalt, and containers. The port also is the home base for a high-speed car and passenger ferry that operates between Milwaukee and Muskegon, Michigan.

Moods of Bradford Beach

Depending on the time of year, Bradford Beach is Party Central—during the annual Beach Jam sports festival, for instance—or a place to enjoy some quiet time, perhaps watching the sun rise before work, taking an evening walk along the shore, or working off the tensions of college life with a quick skate between classes.

Wings over Oshkosh   *(opposite, top and bottom)*

The EAA AirVenture, better known as the EAA Fly-In, is an annual end-of-July event in Oshkosh. Sponsored by the Experimental Aircraft Association, it attracts an international crowd of thousands, including test pilots and astronauts, custom plane builders who arrive in their own creations, and military veterans who want to show their children and grandchildren the planes they flew in.

Up Close and Personal   *(above)*

Exhibits at the EAA AirVenture showcase new developments in aviation technology as well as classic planes, aircraft reproductions, and home-built aircraft. Visitors to the airfield can also witness spectacular air shows that include stunt flying, precision team parachute maneuvers, flyovers of vintage warbirds, and demonstrations by state-of-the-art military planes.

Milwaukee County Zoo *(opposite, above, and right)*

Milwaukee's zoo dates to 1882 as a display of birds and miniature mammals in the city's Washington Park. It moved to its current location in Wauwatosa in 1958. The zoo's two trains are as popular as the animals with many small visitors. The diesel engine has been operating since 1958, when the zoo was located in Washington Park; the steam locomotive was donated twenty years later. The route takes visitors past North American bears, around Lake Evinrude and the koalas and kangaroos of the Australian exhibit, and along the Dairy Complex.

Monkey Island *(opposite, top)*

The inhabitants of the zoo's Monkey Island are Japanese Macaques, also known as Snow Monkeys. Native to the temperate zone rather than the tropics, they are at home in chilly autumn and spring temperatures and delight visitors almost year-round as they swing from the structures in their habitat.

Saving Endangered Wildlife *(opposite, bottom)*

For much of its 120-year history, the Milwaukee County Zoo has worked with zoo-based conservation programs to ensure the survival of endangered species and their natural habitat, including Birds Without Borders. The zoo's Southern Black Rhinoceros, whose species is listed as critically endangered, is one of fewer than 4,000 remaining in the world.

Zoo Puzzle *(above)*

Are zebras white with black stripes, or black with white stripes? These two Plains Zebras, also known as the Common Zebra or Burchell's Zebra, usually inhabit the Milwaukee County Zoo's African savanna habitat along with kudus, impalas, and a common waterbuck. The answer to the question: Scientists think zebras are black with white stripes.

Sixth Street Viaduct

Cables supporting the Sixth Street Viaduct frame Milwaukee's skyline to the northeast. Completed in 2002 to replace a century-old concrete bridge, the viaduct spans the Menomonee River Valley linking downtown and the near South Side. The construction form, called "stayed cable," is a 21st-century version of a suspension bridge and Wisconsin's first bridge of this type for vehicles.

Marquette Slept Here *(left)*

Pere Marquette Park originally occupied a different downtown square; during the nation's Bicentennial, it was relocated several blocks to be closer to the site where priest-explorer Jacques Marquette likely camped in 1670. The bronze statue is a replica of a marble version in the original park; the older statue commemorated Marquette University High School's 1957 centennial.

Riversplash! *(above)*

A three-day downtown party called Riversplash! kicks off the summer festival season in Milwaukee. Held on both sides of the Milwaukee River, but primarily on the west bank, the weekend includes a celebrity paddleboat race across the river, canoe rides for children, evening concerts at a dozen stages throughout the area, and two nights of fireworks.

Circus Smiles *(above and right)*

Wisconsin's International Clown Hall of Fame and Research Center, founded in Delavan and birthplace of the Barnum and Bailey Circus, now is located at State Fair Park. The museum displays clown memorabilia from around the world and maintains a research center for clown history. Members from four major clown organizations nominated the first round of inductees into the Hall of Fame in 1988; since then several dozen more have been inducted from North America, Africa, Europe, and South America.

Garden Galas   *(top and bottom)*

Outdoor concerts by area symphonies and
ensembles draw audiences of thousands to
the Boerner Botanical Gardens in Whitnall
Park each summer. Many families bring picnic
suppers to enjoy before the music begins. A
gazebo-shaped café offers a Sunday brunch
open to the public and is one of several
Boerner sites available for special events such
as family reunions and weddings.

Spring Blossoms

Flowering crabapple trees are at their peak in late April and early May. In addition to gracing parkland, crabapples in pink, deep rose, burgundy, and white line many city streets in the area. Near the end of the blooming season, petals drifting onto the parkways between streets and sidewalks create a temporary carpet of pastel beneath the trees.

Seasonal Display

Boerner Botanical Gardens focuses on displaying ground covers, shrubs, and flowering plants especially suitable for landscaping homes, businesses, and public property. Walking Garden Classes each Wednesday evening in the summer highlight specific categories of plants, and the annual Festival of the Rose highlights the park's extensive rose collection, which includes many All-America selections.

Revitalized Neighborhoods

Just west of downtown, gracious homes built between 1850 and 1915 have been rescued from hard times by homeowners and civic groups, including SoHi, Cold Spring Park, and Concordia Neighborhood Associations. A mural celebrating the area's revitalization was painted by Kate Madigan on a building restored by Chuck Hausmann to house his investment business.

Historic Homes, Renewed Vitality   *(top and bottom)*

This Cream City brick home on West Wells Street was built in 1886 for Adda and David W. Howie. She was an author known internationally for her innovations in dairy farming; he was a coal merchant and Civil War veteran. Now the Manderley Bed and Breakfast Inn, the home has been restored to period elegance by innkeepers Andrew and Marie Parker. Below, the Frederick Pabst Jr. Mansion, completed in 1891 for the son of the founder of the Pabst brewer, now houses Quorum Architects, Inc., which includes historic preservation, adaptive reuse, and applications for historic designation among its services.

Remembering Those Who Served *(above and left)*

The Southeastern Wisconsin Vietnam Veterans Memorial is in Veterans Park on the shoreline just east of downtown Milwaukee. Dedicated in 1991, the three Wausau Red Granite columns symbolize those killed in action, POW's, MIAs, and veterans who returned home. The tallest column is 30 feet high. The memorial is in the same park as the Milwaukee County War Memorial Center.

Riding the Winds *(above and right)*

The spacious Veterans Park, usually windy
because of its proximity to Lake Michigan,
attracts kite flyers from around the state
because of its level grounds and ideal air cur-
rents. For some 30 years it has been the site of
summertime kite festivals, and a New Year's
Day "Cool Fool" event includes ice carving
and free hot chocolate.

Greendale Village

One of three "greenbelt" villages developed nationwide during the 1930s to provide low-income families with jobs and pleasant suburban homes for a reasonable rent, Greendale still offers its 6,000 households urban living within a natural setting. Most owners purchased their homes, now known as Greendale Originals, in 1949. The village has been designated a Historic District and offers walking tours on a regular basis. Participants in a winter festival craft an ice sculpture outside the Village Center; civic buildings and businesses are clustered within walking distance of every home.

Hog Heaven

To motorcycle owners throughout the world, Milwaukee means the home of Harley-Davidson. Incorporated in 1907, the Harley-Davidson Motor Company built its Juneau Avenue factory and headquarters in 1912; the site still serves as the corporate headquarters for Harley-Davidson Inc. A factory in the suburbs and a new 20-acre Harley-Davidson museum in the Menomonee Valley both host tours.

Travel Under Glass

One of Mitchell Park Horticultural Conservatory's three beehive domes displays plants native to the deserts of Africa, Madagascar, and North and South America. A tropical dome includes fruit and nut trees, spice plants, orchids from rain forests around the world, and a waterfall. The third dome features a themed floral display that changes throughout the year.

Flowers in Winter

A conservatory has been on the grounds of
Mitchell Park since 1898; the current facility
was completed in 1967. The beehive-shaped
glass domes are 140 feet across at ground level
and rise 85 feet high. A variety of birds living
in the domes, particularly the tropical dome,
work for their lodging by keeping the insect
population under control.

Resting in History *(opposite)*

The Romanesque chapel was completed in 1899 at the top of "Jesuit Hill," the final resting place for priests and brothers of the Society of Jesus. The hill is both the highest spot in the cemetery and one of the highest in Milwaukee. The chapel was used for Masses on Memorial Day and All Souls' Day until 1950.

Calvary Cemetery *(top)*

This 1890s gatehouse is the entrance to Calvary Cemetery, final resting place of city founder Solomon Juneau, beer baron Frederick Miller, and meat packer Patrick Cudahy. The cemetery also contains memorials to those lost in the 1860 explosion of the steamship *Lady Elgin*; victims included elected officials returning from a speech by presidential candidate Stephen Douglas in Chicago.

Saintly Blessing *(bottom)*

Calvary Cemetery was managed by Capuchin Franciscans, who staffed a nearby church, when it was established in 1857; the cemetery now is maintained by the Milwaukee Catholic archdiocese. A statue of Padre Pio, an Italian Capuchin who was canonized a saint in 2002, raises a hand in blessing near the cemetery chapel.

Forest Home Cemetery *(opposite, above, and right)*

An excursion to the wooded, park-like Forest Home Cemetery was a favorite destination for families, who would bring picnic lunches when they came to visit loved ones' graves. Members of the brewing families Pabst and Schlitz are some of the business and civic leaders interred here, along with Fred Usinger, the city's most famous sausage maker; Broadway legends Alfred Lunt and Lynn Fontanne; and Christopher Sholes, inventor of the typewriter. The brewery headed by Valentin Blatz, who is buried in the neoclassical vault at left, was noted for producing Milwaukee's first bottled beer in 1874.

Military Cemetery

Nearly 40,000 military veterans, including some who served in the Civil War, are
buried at Wood National Cemetery, west of
downtown and near the Miller Park baseball
stadium. The cemetery is named after General
George H. Wood, an early president of the
"board of managers" for the nearby soldiers'
home.

Historic Veterans Facility

Originally known as the National Asylum for Disabled Volunteer Soldiers, this Victorian Gothic soldiers' home was built after the Civil War with the proceeds of a week-long fair sponsored by a Milwaukee women's society. The building now is part of the National Soldiers' Home Historic District on the grounds of the Clement J. Zablocki Veterans Administration Center.

General Mitchell International Airport

Milwaukee County's General Mitchell International Airport is named after U.S. Army Brigadier General William L. "Billy" Mitchell, a World War I aviator who pushed hard his entire career for U.S. air superiority. General Mitchell, who died in 1936, was awarded a posthumous Congressional Medal of Honor after World War II.

Namesake Bomber

The B-25 twin-engine bomber at the south-west corner of the terminal's parking garage is nicknamed the "Mitchell Bomber." B-25 bombers saw action in every theater during World War II. In the background is the airport's 200-foot control tower.

Four-Season Park *(above and left)*

Whitnall Park in the southwest part of
the county includes the Boerner Botanical
Gardens as well as the Wehr Nature Center,
which has five miles of short loop trails rang-
ing through woodland, oak savanna, prairie,
and wetland habitats. A longer natural history
trail connects several habitats, a glacial loop,
and an informal trail around a large duck
pond built by the Civilian Conservation Corps
during the 1930s. At left, a snowboarder en-
joys a long slope in the park that also delights
sledders of all ages.

In-town Forest *(above and right)*

Havenwoods State Forest in northwestern Milwaukee was developed on 237 acres that formerly housed a Cold War missile site. The forest's focus is on environmental education. Its attractions include six miles of hiking and nature study trails through wetland, woods, and grasslands habitats, as well as a limestone-paved bike trail. In winter, a cross-country ski trail is open to the public. A windmill generates power near the forest's Environmental Awareness Center.

Ice Cream with a Plus

Frozen custard, an egg-rich variety of ice cream, came to Milwaukee after the Chicago World's Fair of 1933-34, and never left. Several locally owned custard stands still sell the sweet dessert treat at drive-in restaurants. The exterior of Leon's Frozen Custard, on Milwaukee's south side, was the model for Arnold's Drive-In for the TV series *Happy Days*.

Take Yourself Out to a Ball Game   *(above)*

The red brick façade of Miller Park, home of the Milwaukee Brewers National League baseball team, recalls classic ballparks of the early 20th century. Miller Park replaced County Stadium, the first publicly financed ballpark in the country, where the Brewers– and the Milwaukee Braves– have played since 1953. The stadium was completed in time for Opening Day in 2001.

Miller Park   *(opposite, top and bottom)*

Pedestrian-friendly auto barriers in the form of baseballs define the border of a parking lot near the stadium's clock tower entrance. Because Opening Days in April can be chilly in a Great Lakes city, Miller Park's roof was designed to open for games in temperate weather and close for rain and cold weather. The seven-panel roof can open or retract in ten minutes.

Slice of Ice

The rink at Red Arrow Park draws skaters throughout the winter months. The park is named for the U.S. Army's 32nd Red Arrow Division, the first American unit to pierce the Hindenburg line during World War I; during WWII the division served in the Pacific Theater and accepted the surrender of the Japanese Army in the Philippines.

Motorsport's Pioneer Track   *(top and bottom)*

The oldest continually operating auto race track in the world, the Milwaukee Mile held its first event in 1903, predating the Indianapolis 500 by eight years. In addition to national races, regional events include the Governor's Cup Weekend, when Wisconsin's best stock car drivers take on national champions. Barney Oldfield, Parnelli Jones, the Unsers, A. J. Foyt, the Andrettis, and Dale Earnhardt Jr. all have raced the Milwaukee Mile. The track is located on the grounds of Wisconsin State Fair Park.

Racing to the Future

Renovations of the Milwaukee Mile grand-stand and infield facilities were completed in time to celebrate the track's 100th Anniversary in 2003. Since then, additional improvements have included a state-of-the-art barrier system to enhance the safety of drivers, crews, and spectators and designation of no-smoking areas within the grandstand.

Another Brewing Legacy

Climbing the 60-foot observation tower is popular with visitors of all ages at the Schlitz Audubon Center in Bayside. The 185-acre nature preserve was developed in 1971 on farmland originally purchased to raise grain and stable the horses used by the Joseph Schlitz Brewing Company. Classes, workshops, and summer camps at the Center focus on environmental topics.

Low-Impact Construction *(above)*

Visitors enter the nature preserve through one of the most environmentally sensitive buildings in the nation. Completed in 2003, the Dorothy K. Vallier Environmental Learning Center has operable windows sited to minimize the need for electric lighting, roof overhangs to control summer heat gain, photovoltaic cells to generate electricity, and thick walls for insulation.

Prairie Visitor *(right)*

A monarch butterfly visits a milkweed plant along an Audubon Center trail. There are six miles of trail on the grounds, many of them handicapped accessible; the trails wind through prairie, down a bluff to Lake Michigan, past a glen populated by antique farm machines, over and around four ponds, and up and down a ravine via wooden stairs.

Prairie Trail *(above)*

Off-road bike trails in the Kettle Moraine State
Forest wind through patches of prairie as
well as deep woods. Yellow Coneflower and
Queen Anne's Lace greet these cyclists as they
glide through a patch of midsummer prairie
on one of the Kettle Moraine State Forest's
bike trails.

Autumn Hiking *(opposite, top)*

The Visitor Center in the Northern Unit of
the 50,000-acre Kettle Moraine State Forest is
named for the late U.S. Representative Henry
S. Reuss, who helped establish the 1,000-mile
Ice Age Trail (IAT), a National Scenic Trail
located entirely within Wisconsin. The two
units of the state forest include more than 50
miles of IAT segments.

Prehistoric Landscape *(opposite, bottom)*

Crisp autumn days bring out the colors
of Wisconsin's trees in this scene from the
northern unit of Kettle Moraine State Forest.
The park is named for formations left behind
when the last glacier to cover the northern
United States stopped its advance in Wisconsin, leaving behind ridges formed by gravel,
sand, and boulders.

Glaciated Autumn

The view from the Reuss Visitor Center shows the rolling autumn countryside. Visitors come in buses and cars from all over the Midwest to enjoy the fall colors in Wisconsin, especially along designated Rustic Roads. "Fall color" reports in newspapers and on tourism websites track peak times in various parts of the state.

Après Ski Warm-up *(above)*

Skiers relax after hitting the cross-country trails at Lapham Peak, part of the Kettle Moraine State Forest about 40 miles west of Milwaukee. The area is named after Increase Lapham, considered the father of the U.S. Weather Service for his work to create a storm-warning system to protect Great Lakes shipping.

North Point Lighthouse *(page 128)*

The octagonal Northpoint Lighthouse on Milwaukee's East Side, first lit at sunset on January 10, 1888, is constructed entirely of bolted cast-iron sections. In 1912 the original tower was raised to 74 feet to improve its effectiveness as a navigational beacon. The restored tower and keeper's quarters are now open to the public.